ROCKY REACTIONS!

The Chemistry of **Rocks and Minerals**

Written by William D. Adams

WORLD BOOK

www.worldbook.com

Co-published by agreement between Shi Tu Hui and World Book, Inc.

Shi Tu Hui
Room 1807, Block 1,
#3 West Dawang Road
Chaoyang District, Beijing 100025
P.R. China

World Book, Inc.
180 North LaSalle Street
Suite 900
Chicago, Illinois 60601
USA

© 2026. All rights reserved. This volume may not be reproduced in whole or in part in any form without prior written permission from the publisher.

WORLD BOOK and the GLOBE DEVICE are registered trademarks or trademarks of World Book, Inc.

Library of Congress Control Number: 2025942243

Aha! Academy: Chemistry
ISBN: 978-0-7166-7346-0 (set, hardcover)

Rocky Reactions! The Chemistry of Rocks and Minerals
ISBN: 978-0-7166-7356-9 (hard cover)
ISBN: 978-0-7166-7376-7 (e-book)
ISBN: 978-0-7166-7366-8 (soft cover)

Staff

Editorial

Vice President
Tom Evans

Senior Manager, New Content
Jeff De La Rosa

Senior Curriculum Designer
Caroline Davidson

Curriculum Designer
Mikayla Kightlinger

Content Creator
Joseph P. Cataliotti

Proofreader
Nathalie Strassheim

Indexer
Nathaniel Lindstrom

Graphics and Design

Senior Visual
Communications Designer
Melanie Bender

Designer
Shannon Hagman

Written by William D. Adams

Acknowledgments

The publishers gratefully acknowledge the following sources for photography. All illustrations were prepared by WORLD BOOK unless otherwise noted.

Cover: Micktherocktapper (licensed under CC BY-SA 4.0); Oksana Lyskova/Shutterstock;
Parilov/Shutterstock;Silver Spiral Arts/Shutterstock; Yvonne Baur/Shutterstock

© Cliff (licensed under CC BY-SA 4.0) 29; © David Frazier Photolibrary/Alamy 34, 46; © Design Pics Inc/Alamy 28; © Dorling Kindersley ltd/Alamy 13; © Greenshoots Communications / Alamy 30; © Reuters/Alamy 37; © WorldFoto/Alamy 30; © Bibliothèque interuniversitaire de Santé 10; © Gabriele Burchielli/ (licensed under CC BY 2.0) 28; © KRISTINN MAGNUSSON/Contributor/Getty Images 11; © horst friedrichs/Alamy 27;© cturtletrax/iStock 33; © kerstiny/iStock 34; © Pawel Kajak/iStock 20; James St. John (licensed under CC BY 2.0) 43; Micktherocktapper (licensed under CC BY-SA 4.0) 35; © Jesse Allen/NASA 7; © National Galleries of Scotland 15; Public Domain 32, 33, 39; © Christian Jegou/Science Source 39; Shutterstock 3, 4, 5, 6, 7, 8, 9, 10, 11, 12, 13, 14, 15, 16, 17, 18, 19, 20, 21, 22, 23, 24, 25, 26, 27, 28, 29, 30, 31, 32, 33, 34, 35, 36, 37, 38, 39, 40, 41, 42, 43, 44, 45, 46, 47, 48; Timo Mueller (licensed under CC BY-SA 4.0) 31; © U.S. Geological Survey 36; © WORLD BOOK illustration by Bruce Kerr 15; Yulo1985 (licensed under CC BY-SA 4.0) 34

There is a glossary of terms on page 48. Terms defined in the glossary are in type that looks like *this* on their first appearance on any spread (two facing pages).

Contents

Introduction 4

1 Types of rocks 6
    Forged in fire 8
    Eruptions and lava .10
    Rocky transformations. 12

2 Rock breakdown 14
    Underground wonderland 16
    Soil chemistry 18
    Polluting the soil 20

3 Precious Earth 22
    Minerals 24
    Crystals and gems. .26
    Vital element: gold .28
    Extracting minerals 30
    Vital mineral: borax 32

4 Death in the earth .34
    Fossilization: from death to rock. 36
    The burning rock .38
    Fluid energy 40
    Fossil fuels and the greenhouse effect 42

Rock cycle with crayons 44
Index 46
Glossary 48

Introduction

Did you know that every rock and gem and even the dirt beneath your feet has a story to tell? The chemistry of our planet is full of exciting discoveries, and this book is your guide to exploring the wonders beneath Earth's surface. From the fiery power of volcanoes to the slow formation of precious gems, we'll learn how different elements and compounds shape our planet.

Get ready to dive deep into the world of geology as we uncover how Earth's layers formed and how ancient fossils give us clues about life millions of years ago. You'll learn how such fossil fuels as coal and oil come from the remains of prehistoric living things and how pollution affects the ground and the life in, on, and around it. Along the way, we'll also examine dazzling gemstones, the formation of such precious metals as gold and silver, and how Earth recycles its resources.

Whether you're curious about shiny crystals or ancient fossils, this book will open your eyes to the amazing chemistry happening under your feet!

Chemistry rocks!

TYPES OF ROCKS

Rock is the hard mineral substance that forms the solid part of Earth's crust. Rock is constantly manufactured—and destroyed—on and below Earth's surface. It comes in three types: (1) *igneous rock,* (2) *sedimentary rock,* and (3) *metamorphic rock.*

1. Igneous rock
2. Sedimentary rock
3. Metamorphic rock

The most common type of rock on Earth's surface is sedimentary rock. Sedimentary rock forms when tiny bits of mineral matter or the remains of living things stick together. These sediments may settle out of water, air, or ice! Whoa! Some sedimentary rock forms via the evaporation of water. For example, beds of rock salt—a sedimentary rock— have formed in bays of salty water cut off from the ocean or in saltwater lakes. As the trapped water evaporates, layers of salt crystals are left behind.

You've probably noticed that not all rocks are the same. In fact, rocks come in a dizzying variety—shiny and dull, bumpy and smooth, even heavy and... well...less heavy!

Sedimentary rock covers about three-fourths of Earth's land area and most of the ocean floor. In some places, such as at the mouth of the Mississippi River, sedimentary rocks are more than 40,000 feet (12,000 meters) thick! Geologists estimate that sedimentary rock has been forming for at least 3 ½ billion years.

CAREER CORNER

Do you think rocks rock? Become a geologist! Geology is the study of how planet Earth formed and how it changes. Scientists called geologists study rocks, soils, mountains, volcanoes, rivers, oceans, and other parts of the planet.

Types of rocks

Forged in fire

Igneous rock is formed by the crystallization and hardening of molten material that originates deep within Earth. This material, called magma, is usually a mixture of liquid, gases, and *mineral* crystals. Scientists classify igneous rocks into two groups: extrusive (also called volcanic) and intrusive (also called plutonic). Let's check them out!

Intrusive igneous rock

Intrusive rocks form when magma solidifies beneath Earth's surface. Intrusive igneous rocks are found in underground mines and tunnels or at the surface where exposed by geological uplifting and by erosion. Intrusive rock formations vary from thin sheets to huge, irregular masses. Magma that forms intrusive rocks solidifies relatively slowly, and so most intrusive rocks have relatively large crystals.

The most common type of intrusive rock is granite. Granite is composed mainly of the minerals quartz, alkali feldspar, and plagioclase feldspar. The continents consist largely of granite and of other rocks that are formed from granite.

Granite is common because it forms easily! Experiments have shown that many kinds of rocks yield granite when they melt. Rocks melt in stages, and the minerals that form granite melt first. One of the reasons that granite is so abundant may be the ease with which granitic magma forms.

I'm granite. I love to intrude… because I'm intrusive! Get it?

Extreme heat deep within Earth can break some chemical bonds within rock and cause others to form. Intense heat can even liquify rock! Rock that forms as molten rock cools is called *igneous rock*.

Extrusive igneous rock

Extrusive rocks are formed by magma that reaches Earth's surface along fissures (deep cracks) and at volcanic vents. Extrusive rocks form when magma flows onto the surface of Earth or the floor of the ocean and then cools and hardens. Magma that flows onto the surface is called lava. It may form broad, flat sheets, or it may build up a volcanic shape by repeatedly erupting from a vent.

The most common type of extrusive rock is basalt. Basalt consists mainly of the silicate minerals plagioclase feldspar and pyroxene.

Basalt occurs on volcanic islands and makes up a large part of the oceanic crust, including the mid-ocean mountain ridges. Basalt is also found on continents.

Don't take me for granite! I'm basalt!

DID YOU KNOW?

One form of extrusive igneous rock, called pumice, is full of bubbles and pores. Many pumice stones can float on water! Sometimes, millions of pumice stones will form from an underwater volcano and rise to the surface of the ocean to form floating rafts of pumice!

Types of rocks

Eruptions and lava

When lava first comes to the surface it is red-hot, reaching temperatures 7 to 12 times that of boiling water. Most types of lava cool rapidly, resulting in the formation of rocks composed mainly of microscopic crystals. Some lavas cool so quickly that they form a smooth volcanic glass called obsidian.

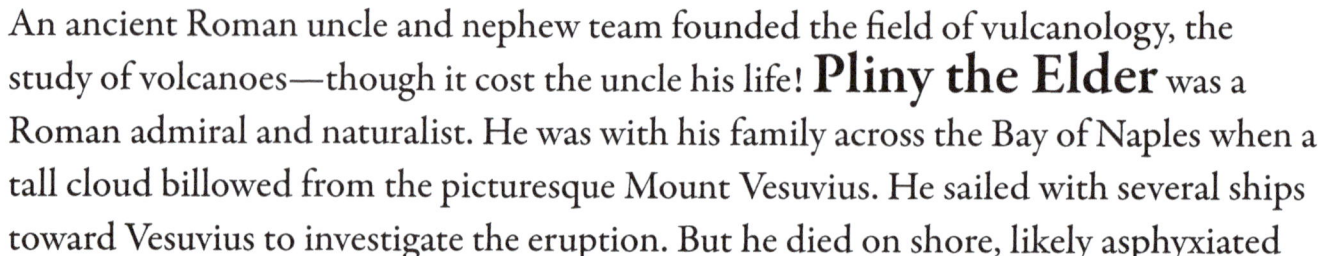

An ancient Roman uncle and nephew team founded the field of vulcanology, the study of volcanoes—though it cost the uncle his life! **Pliny the Elder** was a Roman admiral and naturalist. He was with his family across the Bay of Naples when a tall cloud billowed from the picturesque Mount Vesuvius. He sailed with several ships toward Vesuvius to investigate the eruption. But he died on shore, likely asphyxiated by ash. His nephew, **Pliny the Younger,** stayed behind and survived. He later wrote a detailed account of the eruption by describing his own experiences, collecting his uncle's notes, and interviewing survivors. Vulcanologists call the type of eruption described by the two men a Plinian eruption in their honor. In a Plinian eruption, a towering column of ash spreads out many miles or kilometers in the sky.

Earth's interior can occasionally come to the surface. Sometimes, this rock erupts violently to the surface in some of nature's most awe-inspiring sights.

I'm like a mighty volcano!

Gases from volcanic eruptions include water vapor, carbon dioxide, and sulfur dioxide. Deep underground, the gases are dissolved in magma. As magma rises, the pressure it is under decreases. The gases come out of solution to form bubbles and may eventually escape. It's a bit like opening a bottle of soda!

Why do some volcanoes erupt in towering clouds and others in harmless, bubbling drips? The violence of an eruption depends on the amount of gas dissolved in the magma and the magma's viscosity (thickness). Magmas rich in gas develop many bubbles as they rise to the vent. The bubbles increase the pressure in the vent, causing a more explosive eruption. Viscous magmas resist the expansion of bubbles, leading to a buildup of pressure in the magma. When the pressure of the bubbles finally overcomes the magma's viscosity, an explosive eruption occurs. In more fluid magmas, the bubbles expand without building up excess pressure. The resulting eruptions are relatively mild.

Types of rocks

Rocky transformations

Metamorphic rock forms when heat, pressure, or both cause changes in another type of rock, called the parent rock. One of the changes is the formation of new *minerals*, called recrystallization. The new mineral grains often are larger than the old ones. Flaky materials, such as mica, may crystallize in parallel planes. When this happens, the rock breaks easily along these planes. This characteristic of metamorphic rocks is called rock cleavage.

DID YOU KNOW?

Gneiss is a metamorphic rock derived from granite and other rocks. Whereas granite has speckles and flecks, gneiss features swirls and bands.

Gneiss to meet you!

Deep underground, complex *chemical reactions,* spurred on by heat and pressure, bind rocky building blocks into new compounds. Rock formed this way is called *metamorphic rock.*

Several processes can create metamorphic rock.

Contact Metamorphism

In contact metamorphism, heat produced by nearby magma causes recrystallization.

Regional Metamorphism

In regional metamorphism, both heat and pressure change rock. Pressure comes from the burial of the rocks deep in Earth's crust. Movements in the crust may also affect the rock by deforming it. These movements are often associated with the formation of mountains.

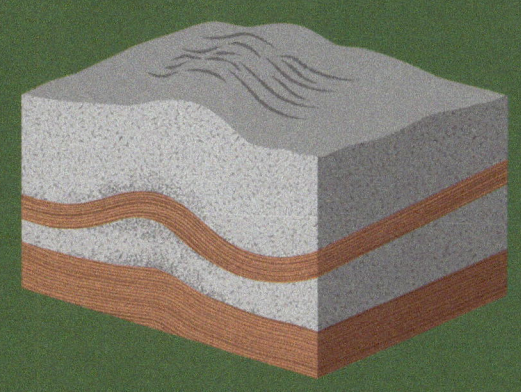

Hydrothermal Metamorphism

In hydrothermal metamorphism, hot water provides heat that changes the rock. The water often also reacts with the rock, causing chemical changes.

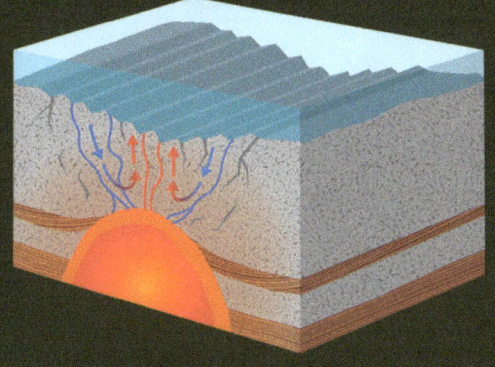

2 ROCK BREAKDOWN

- **Physical weathering usually occurs** as rock breaks down along cracks in the rock or along boundaries between different minerals. Water can work its way into such spaces. The water may then freeze and thaw with the weather. As it does so, it expands and contracts, slowly prying the rock apart. Warming and cooling from day-night temperature cycles and from fires can expand and contract the rock itself, speeding physical weathering.

- **Chemical weathering occurs over time** as exposure to carbon dioxide, oxygen, and water changes the original minerals and dissolves some elements. Chemical weathering may break down rock directly or may weaken rock, helping to break it apart physically.

Rock is solid, but it's far from indestructible. Rock breaks down from the action of wind, water, and chemicals. This breakdown is called *weathering*.

The two basic types of weathering work together. Chemical weathering weakens rock, making it easier to weather physically. Physical weathering, in turn, can expose fresh rock surfaces to chemical weathering. Teamwork!

A process called erosion goes hand-in-hand with weathering. But, it's not the same thing! Erosion is a natural process by which rock and soil are moved from one location to another. Weathering breaks down rock, and erosion moves it somewhere else.

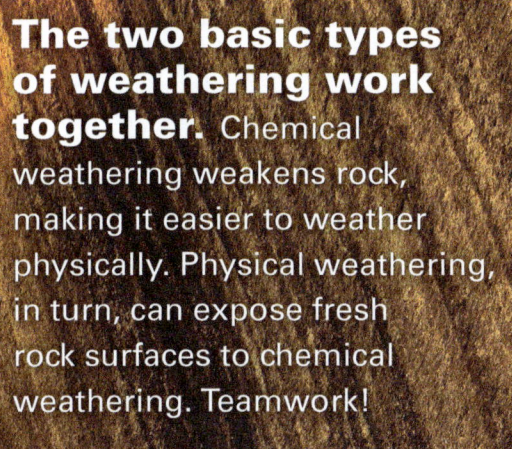

I was put under pressure for my findings!

The Scottish philosopher and chemist **James Hutton** was a pioneer in the field of geology. He studied medicine, but returned home to manage his family's farms. There, Hutton fought soil erosion and studied the folded, jumbled layers of rock on the nearby Scottish coastline. In 1795, he proposed a cycle of weathering and rock formation not too dissimilar from our modern understanding. Hutton's key idea was that heat and pressure deep within Earth drove rock formation. He understood that such processes require many years to play out, making Earth very old. At that time, contradicting the belief in a 6,000-year-old Earth derived from a literal interpretation of the Bible was extremely controversial.

Rock breakdown

Underground wonderland

Most caves are formed in limestone or in a related rock, such as marble or dolomite. Such caves, called solution caves, form as underground water slowly dissolves the rock. This process takes thousands of years! It begins when surface water trickles down through tiny cracks in the rock to a zone that is saturated with water. The topmost level of this saturated zone is called the water table. Water flowing above and below the water table dissolves some of the rock, forming passages, chambers, and pits.

Limestone and similar rock are only slightly soluble in water. However, the water that trickles down from the surface contains carbon dioxide, which has been absorbed from the air and soil above. The carbon dioxide forms a weak acid in the water. An acid is a substance that produces hydrogen cations (H^+) when dissolved in water. Hydrogen cations in the water break the bonds that hold the *minerals* together, turning them into other compounds that are soluble in water. These water-soluble compounds are carried away by the flowing water.

One of the most spectacular examples of chemical weathering is the formation of caves.

Eventually, the water table may drop below the level of the cave. Or, the cave may be raised above the water table by a gradual uplifting of the ground. Most of the water then drains, and air fills the cave. A surface stream may enter the cave and flow through it. The stream may continue to dissolve the rock, enlarging the cave.

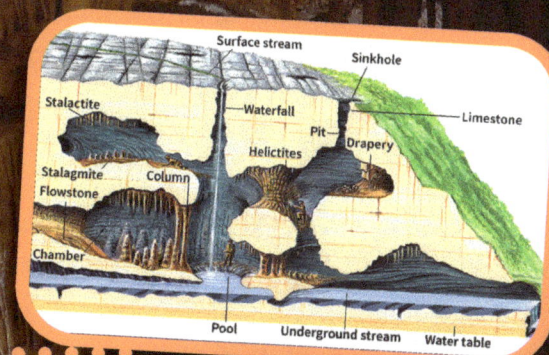

The minerals the water dissolves can crystallize elsewhere inside the cave to form beautiful, oddly shaped deposits called speleothems. Stalactites and stalagmites are the most well-known speleothems, but there are others, including columns, drapery, flowstone, and helictites.

I try to stay grounded.

DID YOU KNOW?

Here's a great way to remember the difference between stalactites and stalagmites: Stala**c**tites are spelled with a **c**, the first letter of ceiling. Stalagmites are spelled with a **g**, the first letter of ground!

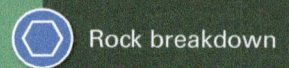

Rock breakdown

Soil chemistry

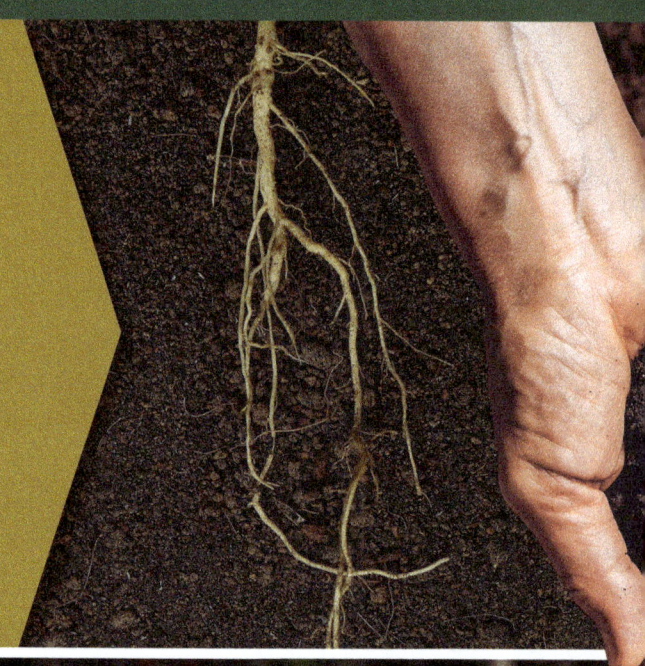

What is soil, and where does it come from? Soil is the mixture of *minerals*, organic matter, and other materials that covers most of Earth's land. The bedrock component of soil is...bedrock! Weathering slowly grinds down solid rock into smaller and smaller pieces, forming the basis of soil. Plants and animals help, too. Many living things produce acids that help break down the rocks. Burrows and roots enable water and air to seep farther into the soil.

DID YOU KNOW?

Soil develops slowly. It may take hundreds of years to produce just 1 inch (2.5 centimeters) of soil!

I help make soil!

Organic matter is an important component of soil. Organic matter consists of dead animal, plant, fungi, and microbe material in various stages of decay. The formation of organic matter is a long process. Organisms called decomposers feed on once-living matter, breaking it down into simpler components. Decomposers include certain bacteria, fungi, and microbes. Other decomposers are invertebrates (animals without backbones), such as earthworms and insects. Ants, beetles, earthworms, and termites also help to mix the soil and create pore spaces for air and water.

Every part of Earth is valuable in one way or another. But perhaps the top few feet or 1 meter is the most important to our existence. Nearly all living things on land depend on soil either directly or indirectly. Life as we know it would not be possible without soil!

Eventually, decomposers produce organic matter called humus (pronounced *HYOO muhs*). Most humus is black or dark brown. It is spongy and holds large amounts of water. Humus binds with clay, protecting the humus from further decomposition. This binding also glues soil particles together to form soil aggregates. Soil aggregates give soil its structure, promoting the formation of pore spaces. Humus makes up only a small percentage of most soils. But, it can greatly increase soil's ability to support plants. The concentration of organic matter in soil typically ranges from 1 to 10 percent.

Warm, humid environments increase the activity of decomposers, enabling them to quickly break down and recycle organic matter. As a result, soil in such areas as tropical rain forests often is poor in nutrients, which are snatched up quickly. In colder climates, organic matter may build up in soils. Northern Asia, Europe, and North America have large areas of soil called peat. Peat contains high concentrations of organic matter, sometimes reaching nearly 100 percent!

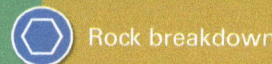
Rock breakdown

Polluting the soil

Soil pollution occurs when soil becomes contaminated with harmful substances. These substances, called pollutants, can become concentrated in plants that grow in the soil. The concentrated pollutants might then poison animals—including people—that eat the plants. Pollutants can also leach (leak) from the soil into nearby waterways. The pollutants may even reach water beneath the surface, contaminating supplies of drinking water. Gross!

Soil pollution can also harm the soil itself by reducing the populations of decomposers that live there. Soil pollution can thus disrupt both decomposition and plant growth. Because much food comes from plants that grow in soil—or from animals that eat those plants—soil pollution can threaten the food supply. Yikes!

When harmful chemicals get into the soil, they can cause serious problems for living things. Such contamination is called soil pollution.

Manufacturing, mining, and other activities produce a variety of industrial wastes that can pollute the soil. These wastes include heavy metals, such as arsenic, lead, and mercury. They also include organic compounds used to make many products. Industrial wastes can enter the soil from leaks in underground pipes and storage tanks. They may also leach into soil from landfills or contaminated bodies of water.

Other soil pollution comes from agricultural agents, including the pesticides and fertilizers used on farms. Pesticides are chemical poisons that can directly harm the beneficial organisms living in the soil and also accumulate in plants. Fertilizers can disrupt normal cycles of decomposition and alter the soil's acidity. These products can also wash into and contaminate nearby waterways.

CURIOUS CONNECTIONS

ECOLOGY What happens in the air affects the ground, too. Burning fossil fuels—such as coal, oil, and natural gas—releases gases into the air. These gases contribute to acid rain, which makes soils more acidic and harms plants and soil organisms. In addition, burning fossil fuels releases nitrogen compounds into the air, which can fall on soil in a process called nitrogen deposition. These compounds cause problems similar to those caused by excessive fertilizers.

3 PRECIOUS EARTH

Rarely can these useful and valuable materials be found at Earth's surface. We've got to dig for them! The process of extracting minerals or other valuable substances from the ground is called mining. Mining involves a lot of heavy machinery, but chemistry does much of the heavy lifting. How? Read on to discover more about Earth's buried treasures!

Earth has more to offer than just soil and rock. Below the surface—sometimes far below—are materials that are incredibly valuable and important to the economy.

I could've been a statue, but I wound up here.

DID YOU KNOW?

People don't just mine for precious metals and gemstones. Quarrying is a specialized mining method that produces stone pieces of a specific size or shape, called dimension stone. People use dimension stone to create decorative items, such as countertops and statues, or structural elements in buildings.

Precious Earth

Minerals

Mineralogists use the term mineral to mean a substance that has all of the four following features:

A mineral is found in nature. Scientists can create many minerallike substances in the laboratory, but only those that also occur naturally are considered minerals. No forgeries allowed!

A mineral has the same chemical makeup wherever it is found. Samples of the mineral halite (rock salt), for example, all contain one atom of sodium (Na) for each atom of chlorine (Cl). All halite all over the world thus has the same chemical formula, NaCl.

The atoms of a mineral are arranged in a regular pattern and form solid units called crystals. The crystals take their shape from the arrangement of the atoms.

A mineral is inorganic—that is, minerals do not include the organic (carbon-based) compounds usually associated with living things. Living things can create a few minerals, however, and minerals serve as an important part of the skeletons and shells of many organisms. For example, the phosphorus-bearing mineral apatite forms an important part of the teeth and bones in many animals.

Let's see those pearly white minerals!

24

We've learned about rock, but what is rock made of? The *atoms* that make up Earth can combine in an unimaginable number of ways. Some of these atoms combine to form the basic building blocks of geology—*minerals*.

A rock is a solid collection of minerals. A rock can be made of a single mineral—for example a rock salt crystal. However, most rocks are made of more than one mineral. Such rocks are called aggregates.

DID YOU KNOW?

Some kinds of minerals are made from ordinary elements that have been thrust into extraordinary environments. Diamonds are made of almost pure carbon—the same element found in living things! But diamonds form in Earth's upper mantle—the zone beneath the crust—where extreme temperatures and pressures heat and squeeze carbon deposits into crystals. Diamonds are later brought to Earth's surface by volcanic activity.

Precious Earth

Crystals and gems

Crystallization is the process by which matter forms crystals. Crystals may form from vapors, solutions, or melts (molten materials). When either temperature or pressure is lowered or evaporation occurs, certain atoms in such substances move close together and join. In most cases, they do so around a crystallization nucleus—an impurity or a tiny piece of crystal consisting of a particle or cluster of atoms. The atoms collect on the nucleus and arrange themselves into structural units called unit cells to form a crystalline solid. A crystal grows by adding atoms to its surfaces in an expanding network of unit cells.

In a few cases, crystals develop smooth, mirrorlike faces. Such crystals are said to be euhedral. Euhedral crystals grow only in spaces where they cannot touch other crystals, so they rarely occur in nature. Most crystals are subhedral—that is, they have poorly formed faces that are rough or pitted. Some crystals, called anhedral crystals, have no faces at all. Most rocks are composed of anhedral crystals.

Not all crystals are rare or valuable, even the euhedral ones. Euhedral quartz crystals can attain gigantic sizes, but quartz is so common that such crystals are nothing more than curiosities. Remember halite? Salt is everywhere, and it doesn't take much to make a nice salt crystal.

A crystal is a solid composed of *atoms* arranged in an orderly pattern. You might think that crystals are rare. But, they're all around you! Most nonliving substances are made up of crystals.

Not all crystals are *minerals*, either. Confused yet? Remember that a mineral has to be inorganic and formed in nature. There are plenty of crystals that don't meet those criteria, such as sugar crystals.

Where do gems fit in? Gems are materials used in jewelry and other ornaments that are beautiful, durable, and rare. Lots of gems are crystals, including diamond, sapphire, and ruby. But nonmineral materials are also made into gemstones, including amber, coral, jet, and pearl.

TECH TIME

Mineral gemstones are rare. Often, mining them is dangerous. Instead, people have developed methods to create gemstones in laboratory settings. Even diamonds can be grown using specialized equipment! Manufacturers can produce large, perfect gemstones in many colors. But, they lack the imperfections that give some gemstones their character.

Precious Earth

Vital element: gold

STATS

Symbol
Au

Atomic number
79

Atomic mass
196.96657

Melting point
1947 °F (1064 °C)

Boiling point
5086 °F (2808 °C)

Gold has a lovely yellow color and a metallic luster. It is also one of the easiest metals to shape. For these reasons, gold has been used to make jewelry and other art objects for thousands of years.

The Varna Necropolis in eastern Bulgaria contains some of the oldest gold objects ever found. The artifacts there are over 6,000 years old!

Gold is usually combined with one or more other metals to form an *alloy*. Gold alloys are less expensive than pure gold, but they may retain valuable properties of the gold. Copper is the metal most commonly alloyed with gold. The karat system, which is usually used for jewelry and ornaments, divides the alloy into 24 parts. One karat (sometimes spelled carat) is equal to one 24th part. Thus, 24-karat gold is pure gold. Jewelry made of 14-karat gold consists of 14 parts gold and 10 parts of some other metal or metals. Don't eat these karats!

14-karat gold

24-karat gold

Gold is a metal prized for its beauty and scarcity. But it is also extremely useful!

Many electrical and electronic devices, including computers, radios, and television sets, have parts made with gold. Gold makes excellent electrical contacts because of its ability to conduct electric current, its high resistance to corrosion, and its ductility (ability to be drawn into wires).

Many countries maintain gold reserves as a way to stabilize their currencies. The United States has the largest gold reserves of any country—more than 8,100 tons (7,300 metric tons)! About half of it is stored in the famous, heavily fortified vault building next to Fort Knox. No trespassing!

CURIOUS CONNECTIONS

MICROSCOPY

Gold is used to capture detailed images of the tiniest objects. Gold coatings are applied to samples to be examined with an electron microscope. An electron microscope is a device that uses a beam of tiny particles called electrons to magnify a specimen. A gold coating prevents the sample from taking on an electric charge, which could ruin the image.

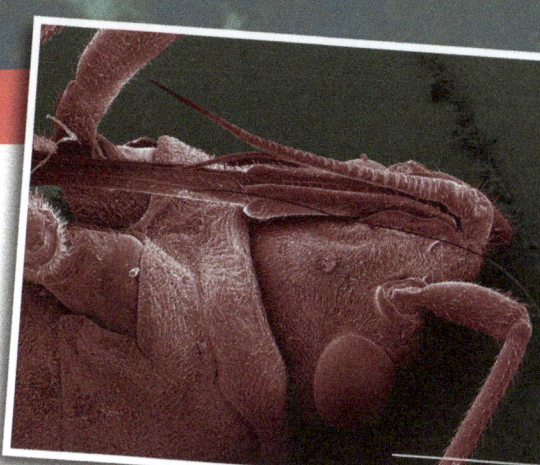

Precious Earth

Extracting minerals

Minerals are rarely found in their native (pure) form. Instead, they are bound up with other minerals or elements in ores. Ore is rock that contains enough of a particular mineral to make it worth mining. Ore deposits often occur within seams in other rocks called veins and in layers known as beds.

Finding big nuggets of pure gold is exceptionally rare. Most gold is extracted from ores with the help of chemistry! Crushed ore is mixed with a cyanide solution, then ground in a device called a ball mill. The resulting slurry, called pulp, flows to a tank bubbled with air. The cyanide and oxygen react with gold in the ore, enabling it to dissolve.

Rice-sized carbon grains are added to the pulp to adsorb (collect) the gold as it dissolves. Filtering the pulp through screens removes the gold-bearing carbon. Treating the carbon with a hot solution of sodium hydroxide and cyanide releases the gold and any adsorbed silver or other metals. That's a lot of chemistry!

Usually, mining is only the first step

in the preparation of a pure *mineral*. Refining the mined material requires lots of chemistry.

Next time you open a canned beverage, think of the chemistry needed to make that can. Powdered bauxite, the most common ore of aluminum, is mixed with a solution of sodium hydroxide and pumped into large tanks called digesters. The digesters heat the mixture under pressure at 300 to 480 °F (150 to 250 °C). Alumina (Al_2O_3) dissolves in the sodium hydroxide solution, forming a solution of sodium aluminate. The other materials in the bauxite remain as solids and are called red mud because of their color. The mixture next passes through a series of tanks in which cloth filters separate the liquid from the solids. The red mud is discarded. But that's not the end! The sodium aluminate solution goes through several more stages dissolving, stirring, and baking to be converted into pure aluminum. Phew!

I'm a long way from the bauxite mine!

TECH TIME

Mining can leave some nasty side effects. The red mud left behind in the processing of bauxite is extremely toxic. It must be held in retention ponds, which can overflow or burst. However, researchers in Germany have discovered a way to extract useful iron from red mud. Red mud can be as much as half iron oxide by weight. The researchers passed red mud through a powerful electric arc furnace. Pure iron nodules appeared within the red mud! The process reduced the volume of red mud, rather than eliminating it entirely. But, the extracted iron could be used in place of mining new iron, reducing the need for further toxic mining.

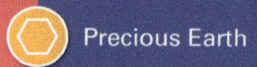
Precious Earth

Vital mineral: borax

STATS

Chemical formula
$B_4H_{20}Na_2O_{17}$

Names
borax, borax decahydrate, sodium borate

Density
1.73 g/cm³

Melting point
167 °F (75 °C)

Boiling point
608 °F (1126 °C)

Borax is a workhorse industrial chemical. It doesn't get a lot of recognition, but it is used in all kinds of products, including glazes for ceramics, fire retardants, wood protectants, strong glass, adhesives—and slime!

Not everything mined is as flashy as gold or diamonds. But other minerals can still be useful! Borax is mined as an unassuming white crystal, but it has thousands of uses!

Borax is a household cleaning champion! Added to laundry detergent, it keeps enzymes in the detergent from interfering with one another, enabling the detergent to work better.

It can also be used as a household pesticide, especially for ants. Mix one part borax with one part sugar and spread it in areas where ants are found. The ants can't tell the difference between the borax and the sugar! They take the borax back to their nest and feed it to the queen and developing ants. The mixture is safe to use on your kitchen counters—borax is one of the safest pesticides available!

Borax was once commonly mined in **Death Valley** in the U.S. state of California—one of the hottest, most inhospitable places on Earth! From 1883 to 1889, mining companies used hauling teams of 20 or more mules and horses. A team hauled two huge wagons packed with borax and supplies and a third tanker wagon. The teams would stop at springs along the way, because they couldn't carry enough water for the whole journey. A filled wagon train would weigh some 30 tons! A railroad line replaced the convoys in 1889, but the inventiveness of the idea and the grit of the drivers—and the mules—made the teams a legend of the Old West!

DEATH IN THE EARTH

When living things die, they usually decompose or are eaten, returning the nutrients in their bodies to the environment. But sometimes, parts or all of them can be buried, giving us unique treasures millions of years later.

When a (formerly) living thing is buried— or even an impression of it is buried—it can turn into a *fossil*. A fossil is the mark or remains of an organism that lived thousands or millions of years ago.

Once-living things aren't just an academic curiosity. They can be transformed into some of the most useful substances on Earth, called fossil fuels. Through *combustion,* fossil fuels release lots of energy that we can harness to power our world.

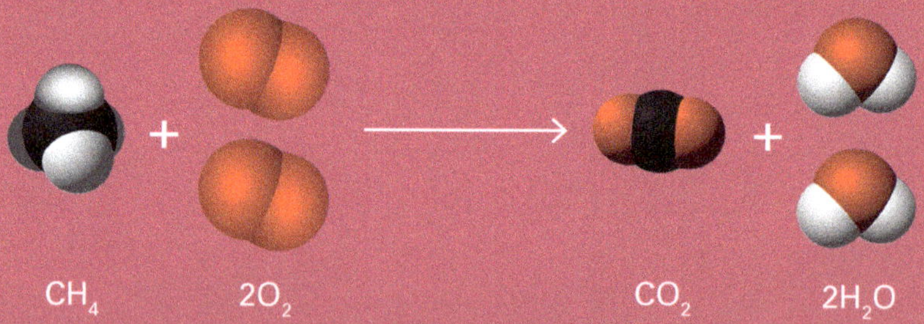

$CH_4 + 2O_2 \longrightarrow CO_2 + 2H_2O$

Burning fossil fuels has damaged the environment, but it has supercharged the quality of life for billions of people. Fossil fuels are also used to make products we enjoy every day! We're moving away from these resources, but they're still vital today.

DID YOU KNOW?

One famous fossil type, called ammonites, were curiosities around the ancient world. We now know they are fossilized shells of sea creatures that resembled the present-day nautilus, but many ancient societies had never seen a nautilus. They interpreted the fossilized shells as divine symbols—or even petrified snakes!

I'm not really a snake, someone carved me this way!

Death in the earth

Fossilization: from death to rock

In some fossils, minerals in the water have totally replaced the original plant or animal part. This process, called replacement, involves two events that happen at the same time: The water dissolves the compounds of the original material, while minerals are deposited in their place. Replacement can duplicate even microscopic details of the original hard part.

Fossils aren't all skulls and bones!

Permineralization or replacement can preserve things like bones, teeth, and shells, but it can also preserve soft tissue. It can even preserve poop! A fossilized poop is called a coprolite.

Fossils may be preserved in other ways, too. Some fossils consist of the preserved form or outline of animal or plant remains. Impressions, also called prints or imprints, are shallow fossil depressions in rock. They form when thin plant or animal parts become buried in sediment and then decay. After the sediment has turned to stone, only the outline of the plant or animal remains preserved.

Many plants and animals became fossilized after water that contained *minerals* soaked into the pores of their original hard parts. This action is called petrifaction. In many such fossils, some or all of the original material remains, but it has been strengthened and preserved by the minerals. This process is called permineralization. The huge tree trunks in petrified forests were preserved by permineralization.

Molds form after hard parts become buried in mud, clay, or other material that turns to stone. Later, water dissolves the buried hard part, leaving a mold—a hollow space in the rock in the shape of the original hard part. A cast forms when water containing dissolved minerals and other fine particles later drains through a mold. The water deposits these substances, which eventually fill the mold, forming a copy of the original hard part. Many seashells are preserved as molds or casts.

Carbonization results when decaying tissues leave behind traces of carbon. In carbonization, a thin, black film of carbon remains in the shape of the organism. Plants, fish, and soft-bodied creatures have been preserved in precise detail via carbonization.

CAREER CORNER

If you like studying fossils, you can be a paleontologist! Paleontologists study fossils to learn what kind of life existed at various times in Earth's history. They also examine how once-living organisms relate to one another and to those alive today. Of course, one target of study is dinosaurs, but there's so much more than that: corals, fish, hairy reptiles, mammals, plants—an amazing variety of forms!

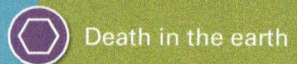 Death in the earth

The burning rock

Coal doesn't form like most rocks. Its formation involves dead plant matter, pressure, heat, and lots of time.

Coal formation starts with an accumulation of dead plant matter. Constant rainfall and a high water table keep the plant material water-logged, limiting normal decay. Under those conditions, thick deposits of dead plant material can build up. The partial decay of plant material produces peat.

The next step in the formation of coal is for the land surface upon which peat accumulates to gradually sink. Such sediments as sand and mud bury the peat as the surface sinks. The buried peat is preserved from decay and erosion, so it can be transformed into coal.

The last step—coalification— changes peat by concentrating carbon and hydrogen and expelling such byproducts as carbon dioxide, methane, and water. The rate at which peat changes to coal depends on temperature and pressure.

Coal is a black or brown rock that can be ignited and burned. As coal burns, it produces energy in the form of heat. It can also help make useful products.

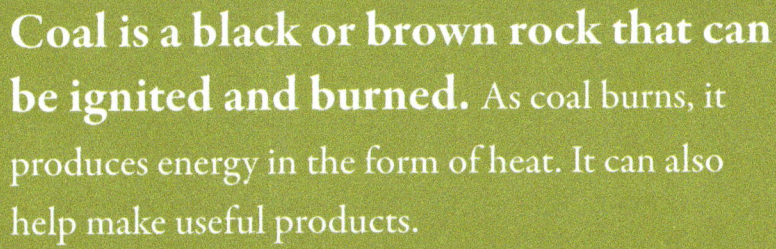

Much coal formed during the Carboniferous Period, from about 360 million to 300 million years ago. That's before the dinosaurs lived! Huge trees grew in Carboniferous swamps and produced heaps of peat-forming matter after they died.

Many substances made from coal serve as raw materials in manufacturing. Coke—a hard, foamlike mass of nearly pure carbon—is the most widely used of these substances. Coke is used primarily to make iron and steel.

The **Industrial Revolution** was a series of changes in manufacturing and society that began in what is now the United Kingdom during the late 1700's. Manufacturers clear cut most of the forests to fuel their new power-hungry machinery and smelt iron. Coal gradually replaced wood—first in steel manufacturing, then in power production. Industrial consumption of coal spread throughout the world. Coal-burning power plants followed the rise of electricity in the early 1900's. But, the U.K.'s love affair with coal has come to an end. Its last coal power plant shut down in 2024, halting the use of coal on the island that started it all.

Death in the earth

Fluid energy

Like coal, petroleum and natural gas developed from once-living matter—the remains of tiny organisms that died hundreds of millions of years ago. Those organisms once lived in the waters of river deltas and along coastlines.

As they died, their remains settled to the sea floor and became trapped in sediment. The remains consisted mostly of water molecules and organic materials rich in carbon and hydrogen. Over time, new layers of sediment piled up.

As the sediments containing the remains became buried deeper and deeper, they were exposed to more intense heat and pressure. These forces compressed the sediment into rock. At the same time, **chemical reactions** changed the organic material into a waxy substance known as kerogen. Further heating caused the kerogen to separate into crude oil and natural gas.

Earth yields more fossil fuels than just coal. Natural gas heats homes and fuels power plants. Petroleum is a component in countless industrial processes, including the creation of gasoline.

Petroleum then traveled through the porous rock in which it formed in a process called migration. Porous rock contains tiny holes, or pores, that allow fluids to flow into and through the rock. Water, which is denser than most petroleum, flowed slowly downward through the porous rock. The water displaced petroleum and forced it to flow upward. Natural gas is less dense than crude oil. Therefore, in deposits where petroleum included undissolved gas, the gas migrated even farther upward. Eventually, the crude oil settled on top of the water. If gas was present, it settled on top of the oil.

I'm kerogen! I still need more heat to transform into oil and gas.

DID YOU KNOW?

Petroleum is not just used to make gasoline and other fuels. It's used as a feedstock to make plastics!

Death in the earth

Fossil fuels and the greenhouse effect

What's the big deal with a little extra carbon dioxide in the air? Carbon dioxide helps trap the sun's heat in the atmosphere, keeping it from radiating back out into space. This effect is called the greenhouse effect; gases that contribute to it are called greenhouse gases. Excess CO_2 released by human activities is warming the planet, leading to climate change, intensifying natural disasters, and other deadly consequences.

What can we do to fight global warming? Such a huge problem must be tackled from many angles, but one idea is to capture CO_2 before it ever reaches the atmosphere. Special devices called scrubbers can capture CO_2 from the exhaust of power plants and factories that burn fossil fuels. Some CO_2 captured at these facilities could be incorporated into products, but most would have to be sequestered (permanently stored). This strategy is called carbon capture and storage (CCS). It's a cool idea, but the technology is expensive. CCS would require government support to be adopted on a large scale.

Think back to how fossil fuels formed. All the carbon within those materials was locked away, deep below the surface. Now that human beings have been extracting it, we've been releasing it into the *atmosphere* as carbon dioxide, or CO_2.

Why not just send all that carbon right back where it came from? Captured CO_2 could be injected underground into natural petroleum reservoirs from which most of the oil or gas has been removed. But, CO_2 injected in this way could escape due to an earthquake or other disruption. Environmental activists also dislike this idea because it's used for enhanced oil recovery, a set of methods aimed at extracting even more fossil fuels.

Here I come to save the day!

TECH TIME

Remember our old friend basalt, the extrusive igneous rock? It could be a climate hero! If CO_2 could be stored in layers of basalt, rock could chemically convert the CO_2 gas into solid salts that would be unlikely to escape.

Rock cycle with crayons

You will need:
- Crayons of different colors
- Crayon sharpener, cheese grater, plastic knife, or other grating device
- Aluminum foil
- Bowl of very hot water (ask an adult for help)

Give it a try
1. Remove the labels from the crayons.
2. Shave or grind some of the crayons down. This represents the weathering process.
3. Pile the shavings on a sheet of aluminum foil and place another sheet on top. Press down firmly. You can stand on the sample to apply more pressure. These pressed-together crayon shavings represent sedimentary rock.
4. Take the pressed crayon shavings and place them in a bowl-shaped piece of aluminum foil. Float the foil on top of the very hot water.
5. Watch as the sample softens. Remove it from the water before it melts. This represents metamorphic rock.
6. Place crayon pieces in a bowl-shaped piece of aluminum foil. Float the foil on top of the very hot water.
7. Allow the crayon pieces to melt entirely. Remove the sample from the water and let it cool. This represents igneous rock.

The rock cycle is cool, but it's hard to study at home. It takes thousands—or even millions—of years for rocks to weather, and rocks melt at thousands of degrees! Let's explore the rock cycle with crayons, instead!

Try this next!

Take a look at some real rocks. Can you try to make crayon copies of them? You can change the size and color of your shavings, how you press together the layers, or even add swirls with a popsicle stick when the wax is soft. See if you can trick your friends with your rock copies!

QUESTION TIME!

Try a different way to grind up the crayons if you can. Are different sizes of particle easier or harder to press together? Do the resulting samples look different?

Index

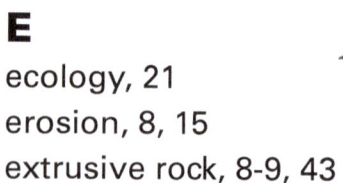

A
alloys, 28
ammonites, 35
atmosphere, 42-43
atoms, 24-27

B
basalt, 9, 43
bauxite, 31
borax, 32-33

C
carbon capture and storage (CCS), 42-43
carbon dioxide, 11, 14, 16, 38, 42-43
Carboniferous Period, 39
carbonization, 37
caves, 16-17
chemical reactions, 13, 30, 40
chemical weathering, 14-15, 17
coal, 21, 38-39
combustion, 34
contact metamorphism, 13
crude oil, 40-41
crystals, 6, 8, 10, 12-13, 17, 24-27, 33

D
Death Valley, 33
diamonds, 25, 27
dimension stone, 23

E
ecology, 21
erosion, 8, 15
extrusive rock, 8-9, 43

F
fossil fuels, 21, 34-35, 38-43
fossils, 5, 34-37

G
gems, 26-27
geology (career), 7
gneiss, 12
gold, 28-30
granite, 8, 12
greenhouse effect, 42

H
Hutton, James, 15
hydrothermal metamorphism, 13

I
igneous rock, 6, 8-9, 43-44
Industrial Revolution, 39
intrusive rock, 8
iron, 31, 39

K
kerogen, 40-41

L
lava, 9-10
limestone, 16

M
magma, 8-9, 11, 13
metamorphic rock, 6, 12-13, 44
microscopes, 29
mining, 21-23, 27, 30-31, 33
molecules, 40

N
natural gas, 21, 40-41

O
obsidian, 10
oil. *See* petroleum
ores, 30-31

P
paleontology (career), 37
peat, 19, 38-39
permineralization, 36-37
petroleum, 21, 40-41, 43
physical weathering, 14-15
Pliny the Elder, 10
Pliny the Younger, 10
pollution, 20-21
pumice, 9

Q
quartz, 8, 26

R
regional metamorphism, 13

S
salt, 6, 24-26
sedimentary rock, 6-7, 40, 44
sediments, 6, 36, 38, 40
soil, 15, 18-21
speleothems, 17
stalactites, 17
stalagmites, 17

V
Vesuvius, 10
volcanoes, 9-11, 25

W
water tables, 16-17, 38
weathering, 14-15, 17-18, 44-45

Glossary

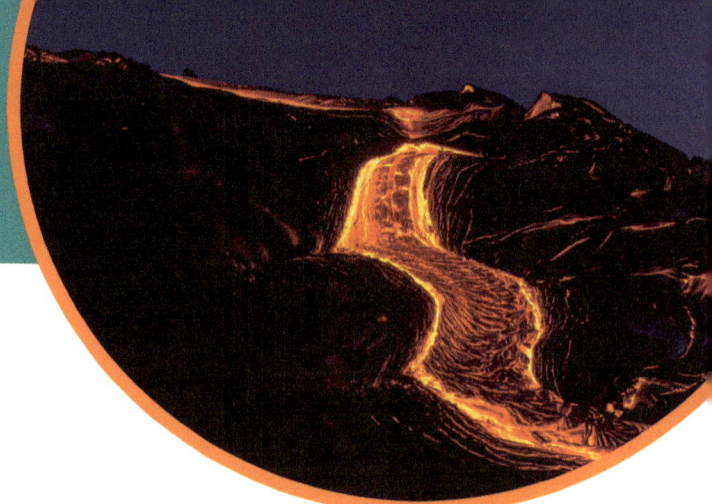

alloy (AL oy)—a mixture of a metal and at least one other element

atmosphere (AT muh sfihr)—the mass of gases that surrounds a planet or moon

atom (AT uhm)—one of the most basic units of matter, consisting of a nucleus (core) of particles called protons and neutrons with tiny particles called electrons moving around the nucleus

chemical reaction (KEHM uh kuhl ree AK shuhn)—a process by which one or more substances are converted into one or more different substances

combustion (kuhm BUHS chuhn)—a chemical reaction that gives off heat and light. Combustion involves the rapid combination of oxygen with a fuel to produce burning.

fossil (FOS uhl)—the preserved mark or remains of an organism that lived thousands or millions of years ago

greenhouse effect (GREEN HOWS uh FEHKT)—a process that traps heat in Earth's or some other planet's atmosphere, causing the surface temperature to rise

igneous rock (IHG nee uhs rok)—a rock type formed by the crystallization and hardening of molten material that originates deep within Earth. This material, called magma, is usually a mixture of liquid, gases, and mineral crystals.

metamorphic rock (MEHT uh MAWR fihk rok)—a type of rock formed when heat or pressure, or both, cause changes in another rock, called the parent rock

mineral—in geology, a naturally occurring inorganic substance in which the atoms are arranged in a regular pattern and form solid units called crystals

molecule (MOL uh kyool)—the smallest particle into which a substance can be divided and still have the chemical identity of the original substance

sedimentary rock (SEHD uh MEHN tuhr ee rok)—a type of rock formed when mineral matter or remains of plants and animals settle out of water or, occasionally, out of air or ice

weathering (WEHTH uhr ihng)—the geological process by which rock is broken down into smaller and smaller pieces

www.ingramcontent.com/pod-product-compliance
Lightning Source LLC
Chambersburg PA
CBHW061255170426
43191CB00041B/2427